I0475116

Writing Serial Fiction In the Real World

A Simple, No-Nonsense Guidebook to Writing and Publishing Episodic eBooks Profitably on Amazon (and Elsewhere.)

Table of Contents

BONUS

Get Access to Writing
and Publishing Materials
from Our Library Collection

Instant Access – Join Here

Click or type into your browser:

http://livesensical.com/go/writingbooks/

PART ONE - WHY SERIALS? WHY NOW?

INTRODUCTION: THIS EPISODE IS BROUGHT TO YOU BY...

The reason I wrote this for you was because I couldn't find a decent ebook on Amazon for this subject. The two I could find there were pathetic (and if you think this one is another, perhaps you should be writing your own. Jump right in, the water's fine...)

So I went out on the Internet and assembled all the research I could to see what and how this subject worked, if it did or not.

Then I compared what I'd learned with what I already knew – and wrote it up for you so you could use it.

You'll see in the Appendix where you can find the same mentors who helped me help you.

I don't pretend to know anything about this subject other than what you see here. So there.

I have published a couple hundred books, so I know how to research and edit and publish. Writing is an endless journey that takes you far, but you never see its end. As you apply yourself, as you push your own envelope, then you improve and find more areas to expand into.

Just to be transparent, my work has been in non-fiction (mostly.) And I got back into studying story structure and plotting, etc. Because the better selling non-fiction works were built on either a narrative, or the "Big Idea" (which is really a collection of short narratives built on the same theme.)

You'll see later in this book my concept for a business plan you can use. How that will work for you is exactly as you understand what I wrote here, as you understand the authors I quoted and linked to, and as you apply this data to work for your own personal scene.

I think it can be made to work, despite all the naysayers we'll encounter soon enough.

It's up to you do decide whether you want to continue on and dive deep into the bottomless pool of your own creativity to surface with new ideas and applications.

Our target is that tiny school of small fish called serials.

Let's see how they're biting today...

WRITING SERIAL FICTION SUCCESSFULLY ISN'T FOR THE FAINT OF HEART

The eternal question for this book is: "Can we write profitable serials for print or ebooks?"

While some writers work at writing for art's sake, the bulk of this would like some monetary gain as well as the fame and glory.

There are two schools of thought and opinion about publishing books and stories online. One school is writing the novel or longish non-fiction work, the other is writing short stories.

A recurring statistical conclusion is that only 300- and 400-page books are making any "real money". Smashwords' founder, Mark Coker, has been releasing his annual reports for some time, based on his own internal number-crunching. They found the trend that longer ebooks sold better and longer than shorter ebooks. He was also the first to find that the $3.99 price range was best for fiction. (The second best price is $2.99.) Unfortunately, Amazon accepts very few ebooks from Smashwords for their catalog. So any Amazon book data was missing - until this year.

Recently, Author Earnings released their own number-crunching results based on bot-scrapes of Amazon's site and found the same thing.

(**Note**: Coker also noted that several of his top sellers were box sets, meaning several books cobbled together. His high average was about 112,000 words, which equates roughly to 450 pages. So this finding may need review.)

What AE also found, incidentally, that most ebook authors didn't sell well, and most ebooks didn't sell well. Amazon has rightly earned the name of "author graveyard." AE says they found 1600 earning a living wage from Amazon, which is over $50K per year. The author community on Amazon speculates that there may be over 500,000 authors publishing there according to Amazon's Author Rank numbers - but only authors that ever sold anything are counted.

(Still, ebooks are a multi-billion dollar industry, and Amazon has 70% of that market per AE. It shows no real sign of disappearing anytime soon.)

Now, not to disappoint you, there are holes in these statistics. (As Mark Twain was credited: "There are lies, damned lies, and statistics.")

Their total sales are just that. They aren't weighted by how many books of a certain page-length exist for sale in any genre or category.

Amazon doesn't categorize their books by length, generally. The bestselling category according to AE is Romance and there are nearly 384,000 Romance Kindle books.

There is a much smaller segment of the Amazon garden called ShortReads. There are just under 59,000 Romance ShortRead ebooks. Under 3,000 of these are less than 12 pages. A 100,000 to one ratio.

The Sweet Spot for Serials

Being able to crank out 2500-word ebooks might be a sweet spot for serials. (Amazon's minimum for accepting any book is 2500 words.)

Note: If you want to scratch this out on a spreadsheet or pad of paper as I lay this out, you might be able to poke holes in this or work out your own best plan...

If you were able to write 2,000 words a day, as Stephen King was doing when he wrote his "On Writing", and you take Amazon's estimate of 250 words per page, that's four pages per day. It would take you approximately 75 days to write a first draft for a 300-page book. At 5 days per week, this would then be 15 weeks, or over a third of a year. With editing and re-writes, you'd add to this.

So figure that you could conceivably crank out two such books a year. Your best price being $3.99, and selling one book per day, at a 70% royalty, this would make you just over $2100 per year after they were both published on Amazon.

If you are writing serials, and have an incredible work-ethic as well as a limitless imagination to bring you new ideas, you could conceivably crank out two stories a week or about 25 stories a year. Short shorts (2500 words) are usually sold at .99 each. At that level, Amazon only grants you 35% royalty. 25 books would then give you over $3100 annually (at one sale per day, our standard.)

Taking a $2.99 sales point for your collecting your short reads into "boxed sets", you'd earn a 70% royalty. Figuring that you collect 8 episodes into a collection and market that as a "season" the years production would give you 3 such collections and nearly another $2300. But you'd also be able to combine those collections into bigger collections (called "boxed sets") at a $3.99 price point, giving you another $1,000. Total would be about $6400 per year.

Which is a better use of your writing time? Two books a year for $2100, or 25 books with collections for $6400? Same amount of time. Different incomes.

To make your $50K income, you either produce 2 books a year for 23 years, or 25 ShortReads a year for nearly 8 years. Your choice. (Yes, you can do *much* better than this with effective marketing.)

OK, that tends to get us all bleary-eyed over numbers and potential earnings.

Your mileage may vary - and less than 100,000 Kindle ebooks (out of well over 3 million) sell more than 1 per day, so this is an optimistic view of potential income. The point is that there is potential here despite these statistics, if possibly inspired by them.

Next, though, is it still true that serials are dead - and doesn't that make all this a worthless mental exercise?

WHERE DID ALL THE SERIALS GO?

Most of the books on Serials cover how Charles Dickens and other early authors made their living publishing in periodicals, and then publishing books based on those installments. However, it's just not done that way anymore. And I cover that history of the serial in the Appendix. From reading that, you might think serials had become extinct as a species. Hardly.

After TV and movies started up, periodicals in print moved started shifting their focus from original fiction over to information and news. What you see these days in magazines devoted to entertainment is more entertainment news than fiction stories. Newspapers are only news. Tabloids are somewhere in between.

Some serialized fiction continued, though. In 1984, Tom Wolfe's "Bonfire of the Vanities" ran in 27 parts in Rolling Stone, where Wolfe was paid around $200,000 for his stories. Later, he heavily revised those articles in creating the standalone novel.

Stephen King tried serializing "The Plant" in 2000, and Michael Faber allowed the Guardian to serialize his "Crimson Petal and the White."

Online, fan fiction has risen in popularity on sites such as FanFiction.net.

More commonly, you'll see work published for free on web-based communities such as Fictionpress.com and Wattpad. Reportedly these books receive as many readers as successfully published novels, some receiving the same numbers as NYT bestsellers.

Of course free doesn't mean profitable, unless you can get those readers to follow you to a paid service.

And I have found in this research that a few people are making serials work on Amazon. But it's tricky, and not well known.

But that's why you're reading this - to see if they can be made to work. It's the question of if you can master this format and make it work for you.

Next, we dive into how the successful ones are really created - if you're up to it...

PART TWO - HOW TO ROLL YOUR OWN SERIAL AND NOT BURN YOUR FINGERS

BUILDING SERIALS IS A DIFFERENT TOOLSET, BUT THE SAME TOOLS.

A story is a story is a story. No matter how short, they all tell it the same way.

This was the conclusion that resulted when I compared the most common and popular plotting techniques with each other.

If you take the Ancient Greek's 3-Act play, then add in our modern versions, such as Blake Snyder's beat system, Joseph Campbell's Heroes Journey, the popular 7-point story structure as explained by Dan Wells, and even Lester Dent's method (he used to churn out the Doc Savage series pulp fiction during the Depression) you'll see that they really all align with each other to describe the same basic method. (See links to these in the Appendix.)

(And after I did all that, I found someone had gone before me. Robert Carlson scratched these all out as well. See link in Appendix.)

Whether a story is short or long, they contain the same basic structure.

What's different in a serial is that they have that structure both in short form for that episode, and in long form for the longer story arcs that the characters are moving through. Coyne covers this as well in his Story Grid , saying that down to the smallest beat (a distinct action a character takes in a scene) up to the overall story, every unit of a story contains these five parts:

- Inciting Incident,
- Complication,
- Crisis,
- Climax,
- Resolution.

Beats add up to Sequences, add up to Episodes, add up to Acts, add up to Story.

Your serial may have chapters in it. Each chapter has those five parts and contributes overall to the 3-Act format your serial is following. Or your serial may just be a short story or even flash fiction (a thousand words or less.)

However, your serials add up into a longer story arc.

The best examples we have these days is using "seasons" as a container to hold serial episodes of continuing stories. Each season has episodes which each may or may not have cliffhangers to get you to watch the next one. It will have each character changing some way or the other. And the readers (viewers) identify with those characters and want to pick up that story where they left off the next week, or the next season.

So you have to write serials while keeping in mind the over-arching changes the characters are going through. Coyne described this as the mini-plots that coincided with the arch-plot for that story.

Interestingly, you'll see these popular shows actually finish off major plots and continue the character's own personal plots. On Stargate, they defeated the main enemy to then get a worse enemy, to ultimately defeat that enemy, only to replace it with an even worse enemy. About that time, the show was canceled and they had to wrap it up with a couple of movies. (Yes they had that much plot left around.)

Star Trek was able to milk several movies and alternate shows out of the original TV series. The character arcs just kept continuing, along with new characters.

Star Wars isn't just a series of movies, but has also taken on alternate story lines through comic books. Of course both DC and Marvel comic book characters from the 50's who have had long runs in that format are now finding new lives in the movies. And others have made the transition to TV from print. Smallville was arguably the longest running serial-based show in that format, tracing Superboy's progress to Superman, with all the love interests and villains along the way.

One story structure to tell them all.

You just have to pick the version that suits you best.

5 DECENT TIPS ON WRITING SERIAL FICTION

Plan, plan, plan.

Having a beat-by-beat organization to where you want your season or series to end up will strengthen your narrative. Such an outline will keep you on track. Threads you set up early will pay off later. There's also the idea that you may want to do a sequel (or even five) so the more long-scale planning you do, the easier your writing will end up.

Take Your Time.

You don't have to wrap up every plot nicely with a bow at the end of a story unit. Having the villain escape can be a nice touch your fans will enjoy (because they know that ultimate justice will be that much greater.) Often a minor sub-plot can turn into your main plot. Realize that your fans will be here for the long haul, so you'll want to string your story along and make it truly an experience.

But don't leave things hanging on forever.

Every story unit should go somewhere definite and enable certain changes for your characters to grow or evolve. The main plot for that episode or chapter should be definite on it's own. The exception would be a part one-part two scene where the audience is included in a longer story arc that can't be told adequately in just a single episode. And you can wrap up threads in a later story that are begun earlier. Plan your work, work your plan, keep your audience involved.

Give your supporting characters the occasional spotlight.

You can create a break in the action by having a minor character take the starring role for that episode. You'll be able to look at things through his viewpoint for awhile as he solves things while your main roles take a break (or are off doing things elsewhere.) But also make sure that it somehow advances the main story arc. One great part is that now your audience has someone else to root for.

Sneak in some fan rewards.

Your long-devoted fans will appreciate having some little inside jokes or obscure references to earlier episodes. Perhaps this is a way to move that little thread along and get it ready for the spotlight a few episodes from now. The truly devoted fans will catch this and be delighted with the nuance of meaning. Also, they'll be able to have something else to discuss in the forums. Hidden meanings can abound, but we really want to make it obvious delight. Keep it simple, though. Crack a joke or make the reference and then back to work on that episode's story arc.

5 MISTAKES TO AVOID WHEN CREATING SERIAL FICTION

You can find truly stupid advice anywhere on anything. The worst is from free downloads or friends and neighbors.

It was the same with this book. As I mentioned, this book was started out of necessity as the only two books on Amazon at the time were truly awful ripoffs. Oh, they had all the smart editorial reviews in all the right places, but when you started reading they just fell apart. Reviews mean nothing if sales suck.

This also happens when you try to study serial fiction. Even the people who have "successfully written" in this format can "say the darnedest things" and not disclose that they have no audience and don't sell well at all. Or that they give all their serial fiction away for free and make their living at a day job, writing only on the weekends.

You also have to watch out for people who wrote serial fiction 8 years ago or talk about programs that have been shelved, like Kindle Serials.

Here's a set of mistakes I've found that recur in the research taken to get this guidebook together:

1. Commit suicide by just jumping right into your serial fiction:

In serial fiction, it's said that the first three chapters (episodes) are the anchor of the story. These are, in the broader story arc, the first act where you set up the story. Use them to establish your characters as you build the world you inhabit. Leave clues, build threads, establish minor story arcs you can build on later. By the third chapter, your ardent fans will be creating the world for you. Give them hints so their imagination can run free. Then they'll tell their friends.

While you should at least create the first three episodes (chapters) before you publish anything, it might be a smart idea to story arc the entire first season (book) so you have everything laid out. This will help your writing go faster.

2. Pantsing only will wreck your serials:
While stream-of-consciousness has helped many authors (particularly the avant-garde like James Joyce and Virginia Woolf) to their own fame, what was hidden in these authors is that they built their stories based on their own lives. So they actually had a framework to follow. While short

stories come out great by pantsing (particularly flash fiction) a serial by definition follows one after the other, building on the preceding.

What holds serials and any story line together is the character arcs, not particularly the episode arcs. You are really following these characters through their various personal changes and they become part of your extended family as you tune into them weekly.

Build your grand arch plot, your character mini-plots, and lay out each episode's particular problem-solving situation broadly. Then you can go pantsing along for each individual episode. But if you pants along from the beginning, with no structure, then very likely you'll wind up eight episodes in with no where to take your dead characters. Plot your future in general terms and then flesh out the details the way that best fits you and your muse.

3. Hang together with your team, or hang separately: Serial writing has been described as only for A-listers. Because the demands on your time are extreme and unending. So having a support team that will edit and proof and walk your dog (occasionally) and allow you to pour your soul into their bottomless ear (more frequently) are all facets of your life as a writer you must allow people to help you with. Build a rudimentary team, if it's only people you trust at Fiverr to continue creating great covers for you.

The alternative is probably inevitable burnout.

4. Don't worry about the characters, they'll show when its ready: Yes we're back to the weird world of pantsing again. You have main characters, and supporting characters. These also have individuals in their lives which need fleshing out, if only slightly. All of these are part of the world you build and present to your reader/viewer. Use Scrivener to keep notes about these, or put them onto a spreadsheet. Motivations, habits, quirks, favorite foods and activities, hidden secrets, interconnections... Keep these noted when you do work up your characters of all types and degrees of separation. They will help you flesh out your threads and give excitement to your readers/viewers as you continue through your serial, its episodes, and its seasons.

5. **Remember your basics:** Got your copy of Strunk's "Elements of Style"? There are rules to this craft which those English teachers tortured you into forgetting. Study your basics and keep hardcopy (as well as digital) versions available and reviewed infrequently. Curl up with them occasionally and brush up on key rules that will make your

writing simpler and more effective. Your readers (and your available time) will bless you.

A SHORT SURVIVAL GUIDE TO SHORT STORIES

Your survival as a writer is at stake.

You need to listen to this, because there are rules and there are Rules.

We've covered how plotting is done, and when pantsing is applicable.

Next is the real mind-creaking internal journey all authors must confront and slay, or run screaming and crying into the night.

Short stories have no real set length.

They follow the rules of story structure, but not always obviously.

Sometimes short stories have no room to be obvious.

But the basics are always there, even for a minor character making a cameo appearance.

And this probably isn't the place to describe all that a short story is and isn't. But it does deserve a mention.

It deserves it's cameo.

The bottom line to success in any story is to appeal to the archetypes we are programmed with from birth, if not before. Opening Scene, Protagonists, Antagonists, Helpers, Mentors, Old World, New World, Ultimate Struggle, Reward, Escape with the Boon, Rebirth, Final Scene.

Try fitting all that into 500 or 1,000 words of flash fiction. Some have to be implied.

Like world building. As Robert Heinlein is quoted, "The door dilated." Instant world. No water to "just add."

OK, maybe not that simple.

But your story has always: Beginning, Middle, End.

Your character goes through both external and internal changes.

There are also always a Hook, Crisis, and a Payoff.

Or you can run through the simpler "story shapes" as Vonnegut called them. (See his video and the study the University of Indiana did on these – links in Appendix.) You'll still have changes in the character(s) of the story depending on the problem they are solving, and their own needs.

The point is that you have to master storytelling. And you can be as verbose as you want, or as miserly.

One approach is to pick your wordage, cut it into four parts, and then work from there. (The center two parts form the second act.) Now you have a few hundred or a few thousand or several thousand words to create the effect you need in each part.

Look up books on Short Stories and work out the basics for yourself. The more you know, the more you've tested for yourself, the more practice applying those basics, the better your work will be.

And, obviously, the easier it will be to market and sell. With a little luck derived from common sense, you can live a very comfortable life as a result.

Your choice. As usual.

HOW DO YOU SELL THESE FRICKIN' THINGS?

Amazon themselves have even given up on Serials, other than the ones left over from their 2012 experiment. Their current page says they "aren't accepting unsolicited manuscripts." And the translation of that means: because they didn't make enough profit to be worth the effort.

The problem could have been in their pricing. Both Mark Coker of Smashwords and the latest Author Earnings report shows that their $1.99 pricing was a dead zone. You simply don't sell much at that price.

Amazon's Serials started as an experiment and lasted maybe 2-3 years before they froze submissions.

A year earlier, they had begun their Kindle Singles. And that seems to have done well for them. In fact, this year, they've expanded it with Kindle Single Classics.

Apparently, it's how the books are offered to the readers. We need to know why Kindle Singles sell well and Kindle Serials didn't.

Jane Friedman wrote a couple of good articles on serials (See Appendix.) In these, she digests the available data by interviewing serial authors. Far from being a complete study, we can still see some data coming to view that we can use.

Right off, the startups who feature serials can't get the distribution or royalties that Kindle is capable of. So we want to work within the existing system.

Readers don't like to be surprised. And they don't like partial books - short reads which were patently sliced out of longer works. Serials need to be written to be serials. Each episode stands on its own, but still contain those longer character arcs. Apparently the best of both worlds is when they pick up an episode and then look to see how they can get the earlier ones in that series. So your writing has to appeal to both audiences.

Mark Coker is no fan of serialization. He's found that people on the whole want to immerse themselves into longer reads, and this also applies to works-in-progress as well as bigger works split smaller. On the other hand, Smashwords customers expect to only buy complete works, so there is a built-in bias that probably works against serials.

With Kindle's separation of Kindle Singles, you can now shop simply for the time-span you have to read in and then buy that length in that genre. So you have people expressly looking for shorter works.

Warnings also show up for people using serialization as a marketing gimmick. This really falls into chunking off larger books with slight editing, instead of honestly writing short fiction which build into a larger compilation.

How to get started can be tough as well. Many serial authors give their earliest episodes away for free to build their audience. This isn't appealing to many authors who need that paycheck right off.

One such way to build audience would be Wattpad, which is designed for works-in-progress, and builds fan bases readily. Several free episodes out there would build into sales for the first collection.

On Kindle, the sales which are happening are where authors are routinely publishing new books in a series. This matches what the Author Earnings reports, especially their Romance presentation. Authors who have more books in a series do better, authors who publish more books per year do better.

All this points to success for serial authors who write specific episodes which as a series which can then be combined into a collections as chapters.

BUILDING YOUR SERIALS FOR SUCCESSFUL SALES

While you start with the end in mind, you also start well in order to end well.

How you structure the book and how well you write the individual episodes monitor how well you will sell. Again, it's quality books produced in volume.

We've heard the horror stories of failure. But we also note that the authors doing this are taking short-cuts and getting caught out.

If you're going to write longer novels, then do that.

But the people writing short stories who master the craft have no problems finding their books sell and continue to sell. Especially when selling their short stories as Kindle ShortReads, and then compiling them into collections and "boxed sets."

Now, let's get some terms straight for this project:

(We're using TV terms as these are easier for those of us raised on weekly dramas instead of Dickens' Pickwick Papers.)

An individual serial short story – episode.

A collection of 16 episodes – season.

A collection of 4 episodes - season part.

The general plan I see at this point is to have a "season collection" available as well as quarters of the seasons as collections.

All of this is designed based on Amazon's general trends and accepted counts.

(Here's where you drag out a yellow pad or spreadsheet to follow along, or skip to the Appendix to see it that way.)

Episodes are at least 2500 words, to be published as Kindle ShortReads.

Season parts are at about 10,000 words (4 episodes) as this is just above the minimum needed to produce CreateSpace paperbacks at 32 pages each. (Yes, that's thin. Easy to slip into a purse or briefcase, even a wide pocket.)

The full season is 16 episodes, as that is pretty close to industry standards for TV series, and also works with the 3 Act structure (1st Act 4, 2nd Act 4+4, 3rd Act 4.) This can give you another paperback, and is thick enough for CreateSpace to print on the spine big enough for people to read.

Why 4 episodes as the minimum collection? Because you can crank that much out in a week. 4 episodes and a mini-collection.

With me so far?

OK, because it gets more intense (and yes, I have this gridded out in the Appendix.)

So that means you are cranking out a season every 4 weeks.

And each week you have not only 4 episodes, but also a season part, which becomes a thin paperback.

In two months. you have 2 seasons done. In 4 months, you have four seasons done and can then compile them into a 250+ page paperback, suitable to shipping to libraries and wholesalers. The 250 page count is the upper end of where the cost-effectiveness of any Print On Demand books (like CreateSpace) still competes with short-run presses. This is also thick enough for libraries to take them, as you can now clearly see the title on the shelf.

By the end of a year's worth of work (technically, 48 weeks) you have 12 seasons created. Each of these are in their own collection and thin paperback. You also have 3 250-page books, 48 thin episode paperbacks, 48 part-episode collections, 192 short reads.

Meaning that in one year, you've just created a publishing empire and given your fans something to look forward to.

Pricing these is pretty standard by Amazon terms:

- Individual episodes: .99

- Weekly part-seasons: 2.99

- Seasons: 3.99

- Multiple seasons will then be higher, depending on page counts, but probably stick at 4.99 for 2 and 4-season sets.

(As an interesting note, if you can get a year of this output to sell one per day, you then get just over $72K annually, which makes this well over minimally viable. Note: this is just ebooks. Added sales from print and audio, plus other marketing you can do may raise this higher. Again, this isn't any promised payout - your own mileage will vary.)

Delivery is something you'll need to play with. If you could publish 4 episodes per week, a person could get through these every day, or binge by getting the part-episode collection for the weekend. This would probably do great for thrillers and romances. You might be able to skip a week in between episodes to tweak demand for your stories.

The production strategy would be to get and keep at least one episode ahead, so you have time to edit the serials into shape and keep the story-arcs moving well. You can also then go back and drop hints and reminders into the episodes, particularly in order to set up the next season as you write it.

Sure, this is involved, but we want our readers challenged. They like it that way.

Something to solve in this is to get the audio coming out with the print editions. Remember that you can sell the episodes as individual MP3's, or give them away as a podcast (maybe smarter.) Then sell the collected works for people to buy as a download or CD.

The point is to immerse your audience in these episodes and start expecting to see what is happening with their favorite characters as the series continues.

What you do have to realize is that you're committing your life to this series for the next year. And you are going to have to tap deep to get 192 short stories written during that time.

But that's a lot of plates spinning all at once, a lot of balls in the air.

Most people can't.

You've been warned.

A SHORT NOTE ON MARKETING AND ADVERTISING FOR SERIALS

Mostly, stick with running ads for the season collections.

Reason being, higher priced collections will enable your Facebook advertising to pay for itself.

Also, this means you can run a campaign for a month before starting your next campaign. Toward Christmas time, you'd then come up with a super-binder of multiple seasons available so people can have complete collections. But that is different marketing.

Just wanted to leave you a note before we get any further.

What? You haven't gotten training on Facebook ads yet? Check with Mark Dawson or start hunting up this data on your own...

HOW TO STUDY SUCCESSFUL TV SERIALS TO WRITE BETTER

Of course, I found this out from someone else. But writers have been studying/copying/stealing from other authors forever.

In this case, it's Geoff Shaw who has a course on Udemy (see Appendix.)

He points out that the hour-long TV episode is nicely chunked up into four 12-minute sections so that they can run ads in between.

This is also how the 3 Act story structure works.

- Act 1 - first 12 minutes.

- Act 2a - second 12 minutes.

- Act 2b - third 12 minutes.

- Act 3 - final 12 minutes.

You'll also see from where we covered story structures, that most follow this break down. If you check Lester Dent's formula for how he treats his hero in the Doc Savage pulps, you'll see that it's all in four sections, getting far more intense every time.

This also predicts your page count. Starting from an 8,000 word goal, each of those sections is 2,000 words long. A 2500-word goal would have 625-word sections. And if you write it so that there is a break in the action just before a commercial, then it will seem normal to you.

Now to save you time, so you don't have to re-watch these episodes, you can look them up on IMDb for full plot treatments. This would also be a good time to study through the overall character arcs for the series, season by season. That will be good homework to build an over all story arc as well as maintaining the individual character arcs.

Another video you should watch is to look up the 7-point system as described by Dan Wells. In this, he dissects the Matrix (starting about the third video) and shows how character arcs can be integrated into the overall story arc as it moves along.

Yes, this is a lot of work.

Yes, I told you this isn't pantsing.

But do you want to work smart or hard?

PART THREE - ARE SERIALS SOMETHING TO BUILD AT HOME?

THE RISE AND FAILURE OF POPULAR SERIALS

Now we've found how writing profitable serials is all but impossible.

The worst model you can use is trying to compare yourself to Charles Dickens. In those days, books were very expensive and the populace mostly illiterate. The inexpensive periodicals which published serials in those days actually were teaching people to read and appreciate stories. There was no competition from TV or radio or movies or streaming on-demand video.

The stories you are writing now have to grab a reader's interest and suck them into the vortex of action before they know what hit them.

What you won't be doing is to study the form and language of long-dead authors in order to impress our current generations with classic style and grammar.

What you will need to do is to master your own work-ethic and talent to find new and exciting ways to stand out among the wannabes and also-rans.

Your secret weapon is to study the most popular serials of all time - which are TV series which have run multiple years. Most of these have had different directors, different producers, and the casts have changed out. (Stargate killed off one of its main characters several times over the years, only to revive him again and again.)

The story is what lived. The screenwriters would change, but the story had a life of its own. Until it finally ran its course – or not.

Yes, lousy writing and stupid acting has killed TV serials. If a written serial isn't popular, it is the fault of the writer alone. (While there are also stupid network decisions, such as the premature burial of "Firefly".)

There is life in any story, says Chris Vogler in his "Writer's Journey." By his Third Edition, he'd added an essay in the appendix titled "Stories Are Alive" where he traces how stories continue to have lives of their own after they make their original birth into our culture. They can reborn, reworked, recast, refilmed, rewritten. The story can change or it can stay the same. But it's alive and out there.

So don't think your serial is dead because no one loves it. Even if you hated it yourself, but had to get it out of your system so that your muse would let you sleep at night. Perhaps it is an evil monster. But even monsters have a theme, have a mission, have a reason for existing.

As you write a serial, it simply has to appeal to the archetype-shorthand that we all use to understand the world around us. Vogler's book is an excellent introduction to that shorthand, better even than Joseph Campbell's original tome. Because it was written by a writer for writers.

You are the midwife, the go-between for the story you bring to life.

You can always go back and make it better, re-title it, get new covers made, get new reviews, republish it on different platforms, lower the price, raise the price... You can do anything and everything you can to breathe life into it and give it wings to find its own way in the world.

It won't be for want of trying.

The better your skill (which comes with study and practice) the easier this will become for later stories.

And there is even another option: several artists and writers actually only ever paint or write the same story over and over and over. People buy these and never get tired of them.

Because people want symbols and stories in their lives to help them make sense of everything. They want to reach the point where their emotional needs and rational wants match. At that point they buy. At that point, they have something that helps them "make sense" out of this sometimes chaotic and confusing world.

You then have a hit on your hands.

And then you start to work on the next one.

ARE SERIALS SIMPLY IMPOSSIBLE TO WRITE, MARKET, AND PROFIT?

It just might be that you've read this far only to see that writing serials isn't for you.

Serials are hard to write, probably harder than novels. Certainly harder than non-fiction.

But if you think about it, don't all chapters in a book somewhat follow the pattern of a serial?

The trick is that they aren't written to fit the dual duty of both standalone episode and mortar between two bricks in the wall. Good serials are. Novels split up into pieces don't.

And this is probably what you are running up against.

Serials are hard to write. There are no shortcuts.

Serials make different demands on your time. They are a marathon, not a sprint. Short stories are a foot race. One and done. Serials have mile after mile after mile. And on the Boston Marathon, there is a section known as Heartbreak Hill, where the steady upward climb has killed more hopes of potential winners than any other section. (Not too oddly, that matches the part of the Three Acts as a Crisis.)

But for the real writer, the world can now be understood as a Serial. You have seasons of episodes and your journey continues, or a new one starts.

As you study and practice, your writing should become easier.

There is an old story of a person passed over for promotion. When he asked why this other person (who had been at the firm less time than he had) was more qualified, he was told that he had more experience.

He then retorted, "But I've had more years at the job."

And was told, "And you've done the same job for all that time, over and over. You relived the same experience during that time. The other guy sought out different experiences and learned more tools and solutions he could use to solve more problems for the company. That's why he got the job."

The shortcutter doesn't make it at anything until they realize they need to learn and apply the basics.

It doesn't help in our world that some shortcutters can make millions "over night." What you don't see is where they eventually lose it all, or the miserable lives (of the rich) they lead because they try to short-cut everything in their lives. You only see their brief moment in the sun.

There are rules and there are Rules. There are the law of human societies and there are Universal Laws. Some can be bent or broken without consequence, if there is no one to enforce them. The others are policed by greater forces than you can imagine. And those stories are told through the ages.

The moral: Short cut and fail. Study, learn, know your crafts of writing and marketing. Then you succeed to the degree you have faith in yourself and apply what you learn. And you persist on your own journey.

AND JUST WHEN YOU FELT LIKE GIVING UP...

The darkest parts are just before the dawn.

And any writer can "hit the wall" occasionally on any project.

I've tried here to tell you some ideas you can use to avoid this problem. For it isn't a cliché - it's very real.

Implied or implicit, it's in every story you write. It's an archetypical situation that is met by any hero(ine) on any journey.

And yet, you know you just can't do this stuff. You've tried and failed, and tried again and failed again.

Maybe thousands of times, like Edison and his light bulb experiments. Or the 39 times before WD-40 was perfected.

I'm here to tell you now: persist.

Eventually, you'll have a breakthrough. The clouds will part (if only slightly) and the world will get a bit more rosy as everything starts to work out.

Yes, serials can be hard. They can be impossible to write. And you can wind up facing a plot hole that condemns your project to a screeching or quiet halt.

Do you then re-write?

Do you then go back to the editor and beg for help?

Do you shelve the project and maybe never pick it up again for years or ever?

This is what faces you now.

Maybe you took a shortcut. Time to go back and un-do that.

Maybe you pantsed when you should have planned. Time to go back and do that, then come forward from there.

Maybe you do need to do some massive re-writes. (Sigh.)

What do you do?

Whatever you decide, it's between you and your muse and your audience.

If you are truly willing to "kill your darling" then you can yet have success with this.

No, eating crow doesn't taste good regardless of the seasoning. Pride goes before a fall, but the only problem with falling is when you don't get back up (as Mary Pickford used to say.)

PART FOUR – ONE SERIAL TO RULE THEM ALL

HOW YOU COULD WRITE YOUR OWN SERIAL SUCCESS STORY

If you're reading this, you have courage beyond most writers. You weren't scared off by all the warnings, trolls, and great gray whales.

It's not impossible to write successful serials.

It does take planning, and nothing succeeds without your putting your best into it. That means work.

0. Setup

Schedule your day so you spend your most inspired time writing, and an equal amount of time marketing.

Ensure you aren't interrupted while you are supposed to be writing.

Set daily word goals and make them.

Read books in your genre any spare moments otherwise.

1. Book Structure

Decide on your page count. Determine if you how many days of regular writing each first draft is going to take.

Work out your book structure and the arch-plot for the series itself. (Each individual episode will have its own arch plot.) Map out a season's worth of episodes in the rough.

Work out your character's mini-plots

Work out the rest of the details, such as world-building, series theme (and each episode theme).

Get these all down on a spreadsheet.

2. For each episode:

Set up a spreadsheet that grids out what happens when. Your character mini-plots will interact during this, but this is in the main just for that episode's arch-plot.

Set your arcs, your plots, your interactions.

Then pants it out, episode, by episode.

The next day, use Coyne's Story Grid to self-edit your book into shape - or send it out to an editor and start on the next episode.

Note: if you're doing four episodes a week, it might be better to edit a week's production all at one go.

3. Send off for the cover (preferable) or do it yourself. You may set up several covers in a batch for that season, along with the season collection cover, and those of the audiobooks and CD's, getting a bulk rate.

4. Do the needed edits, including any re-writing.

5. Get it proofed.

6. Finish all the episodes and combine them into the season (collection).

7. Send each episode out to your advance review team for their input.

8. Publish each episode on a schedule and alert your review team so they can post an honest review on Amazon.

Set your episodes to come out weekly until complete.

9. Publish your season as a collection, and also as a paperback on both Lulu.com and CreateSpace.

Select global distribution on Lulu and order the physical proof. This gets you into Ingram as a wholesaler. Price your CreateSpace book competitively with your Lulu book to get best royalties. Then set up a 50% discount (if you like) on Lulu. Send these links to your review team as a bonus.

10. Get your audiobooks created and published through Author's Republic.

Also publish these through CDBaby to get into all possible music stores, as well as on Amazon as CD (spoken word album.)

- - - -

Meanwhile, you've started your marketing for the book with any online ads, getting into book review blogs, and being interviewed by podcasters and local radio.

Also, you've started in on your next season by mapping out the arch-plot and continuing the character mini-plots through.

After that, just keep rinsing and repeating.

- - - -

This is just the broad strokes, but gives you an idea of what's ahead of you. Book publishing and marketing are covered in many other good books, and are quite beyond the scope of this simple edition.

See Appendix for those I recommend.

Your success is, and always has been, completely up to you.

THE NEEDS AND WANTS OF THE SERIAL WRITER

You've seen this in your story structure studies: every character in your story has a need and a want.

The want is the object they are chasing, their goal, and for the antagonist, Hitchcock's "MacGuffin."

The need is internal, the unmet emotion or feeling the character is lacking. Whether they know it or not.

You as the author, want to understand how to write serials and earn extra income (or make a living) doing this.

You as the author may need many things that success in this field will give you. For some, it's the relief of your muse leaving you alone for awhile (until that next inspiration strikes.) For others, it's the cathartic relief of having the story take on it's own life, as you've written parts of yourself into it. Now you can let your emotional past go. Adieu. Goodbye.

Some people can pursue the gossamer goal of public adoration and approval.

A piece of advice here: define these things for yourself.

At this point of this short book, you have all the tools you need to write successful serials forever. What is left is for you to internalize these and practice until they become second nature.

Like any performance art, there are only so many bad performances in you. But enticing the good and excellent ones out depends on learning from your mistakes and seeing honest reviews of your craft.

Then your wants and needs can all be fulfilled.

At that point, pick out some new goal and get going on your next journey.

THE SERIAL WRITER RODE OFF INTO THE SUNSET, SINGING...

At least that's how the old western serials used to go. Tex Ritter, the Lone Ranger, Gene Autry, Roy Rogers, and all those cowpokes. (And how about Annie Oakley?)

The darkest hours are behind you - for now.

You may yet face the most powerful antagonist ever. But that episode is around the corner, not today.

Hidden in this book are some strategies and tactics which can make your serial-writing easier and more profitable. As well, you'll need to do additional hours of study on related books and materials. I've left you plenty of links within the book and in the Appendix to follow.

For me, it's getting this edited into shape and published and promoted. Since you are reading this now, it's probable that I was successful in this.

I am on my own journey to improve my own writing, publishing, and marketing. The life we both seek, apparently, is greater ease at doing what we most love.

For both of us, this stage of the journey is nearly complete.

So I wish both of us the best of luck.

PART FIVE - APPENDIX

WRITING AND PUBLISHING LINKS:

Writing Links:

A Plot Grid - http://calm.li/plotgrid

Table of Story Structures by Robert Carlson - http://calm.li/storygridpix

Vonnegut's Shapes of Stories - https://www.youtube.com/watch?v=oP3c1h8v2ZQ

Six Emotional Story Arcs - http://calm.li/sixplotarcs

Blake Snyder's "Save the Cat" - http://amazon.com/dp/B00340ESIS

Dan Well's 7-point Story Structure (5 Videos) - https://www.youtube.com/watch?v=KcmiqQ9NpPE

Smashwords' Mark Coker Annual Reports - http://blog.smashwords.com/2016/04/2016survey-how-to-publish-and-sell-ebooks.html

Author Earnings 2016 Report - http://authorearnings.com/report/may-2016-report/

Author Earnings Romance Report - http://authorearnings.com/2016-rwa-pan-presentation/

How many authors on Amazon - KDP Community - https://kdp.amazon.com/community/thread.jspa?messageID=883474

Stephen King "On Writing" - https://www.amazon.com/dp/B000FC0SIM/

Lester Dent's Master Fiction Plot - http://www.paper-dragon.com/1939/dent.html

Shawn Coyne "Story Grid" - http://www.storygrid.com/

William Strunk Jr. "Elements of Style" - https://www.amazon.com/dp/153069535X

Mark Dawson Facebook Ads Course - http://www.selfpublishingformula.com/

Geoff Shaw's Reverse Engineering Riveting Fiction & Write Best Selling Books - https://www.udemy.com/reverse-engineer-riveting-fiction-write-best-selling-books/

Geoff Shaw's How to Succeed with Kindle Short Reads - https://www.udemy.com/how-to-succeed-with-kindle-short-reads/

Internet Movie Database - http://www.imdb.com/

Wikipedia - "Binge Watching" - https://en.wikipedia.org/wiki/Binge-watching

Wikipedia - "Serial – Literature" - https://en.wikipedia.org/wiki/Serial_(literature

Wikipedia - "Soap Opera" - https://en.wikipedia.org/wiki/Soap_opera

Publishing Links:

These are all Print On Demand for self-publishing. As mentioned, you can get these produced more cheaply through a short-run printer, but will have a higher cost and a lot more books to sell.

Lulu.com - www.lulu.com/create/books - tells you their printing costs.

Createspace.com - https://www.createspace.com/Products/Book/#content6 - tells you their printing costs.

Lulu.com vs Createspace.com costs - http://www.lugaru.com/lulucalc.html This site gives you a comparison between the two. A little dated, but looks fairly accurate.

You can also publish your book on each of these partially to get to their pricing calculators - but the above link gives you a roughly accurate idea.

IngramSpark - http://www.ingramspark.com/

Annual fees to maintain your Ingram connection (which neither Lulu nor Createspace have.)

Lightning Source - https://www.lightningsource.com/shippingcalc.aspx

A bit involved as a high-end POD publisher - also gets into Ingram's system. Compare their prices in bulk to CS and Lulu.

 The Catalog Block - what you have on your copyright page to get into libraries and wholesalers: www.dgiinc.com/pcip/

Other books in this series

Visit http://livesensical.com/book-series/publishing-and-writing/ Available on Amazon, Lulu, and as Pay What You Want

Really Simple Writing & Publishing

Learn How to Write, Design, Format, Upload, and Sell Your Own Book for Low Cost or Free. (http://livesensical.com/book/really-simple-writing-publishing/)

J'APE: Just Another Publicity Excuse

How to Publish Your (Kindle) Book for Shameless Self-Promotion and Profit (http://livesensical.com/book/jape-just-another-publicity-excuse-parody-celebrity-self-publishing/)

Publish. Profit. Independence.

How to Earn Extra Income and Financial Freedom by Publishing on Your Own (http://livesensical.com/book/publish-profit-independence/)

How to Write Less and Profit More

A Rich Adventure in Short Read Kindle Publishing (http://livesensical.com/book/write-less-profit-rich-adventure-short-read-kindle-publishing/)

Writing Serial Fiction in the Real World

A Simple, Tongue-in-Cheek Guide to Writing and Publishing Episodic eBooks for Profit on Amazon (and Elsewhere.) (http://livesensical.com/book/writing-serial-fiction-real-world/)

How to Help Librarians Fall in Love With Your Self-Published Book

...and Get More Sales When They Do. (http://livesensical.com/book/help-librarians-love-book/)

Cracking the Kindle Sales Code

How to Search Engine Optimize Your Titles and Descriptions so Amazon Promotes Your Book and Recommends Buyers to You at No Cost (http://livesensical.com/book/cracking-kindle-sales-code/)

Your Kindle Booksales Blueprint

How to Break Out of the No-Sales Amazon Self-Publishing Basement and Routinely Start Getting Regular Passive Income From Your Kindle Booksales Without Added Expense or Tricks (http://livesensical.com/book/kindle-booksales-blueprint/)

Related Writing Texts Published by Midwest Journal Press

See: http://livesensical.com/go/writing-refs/

Carolyn Wells' *Mystery Story Technique for Writers*

Creating Your Children's Book by Thrive Learning Institute Library

Technique of Fiction Writing by Robert Saunders Dowst

Becoming the Fiction Storyteller of Your Dreams by Robert C. Worstell, Dorothea Brande, and Marie Shedlock

Becoming a Writer, by Dorothea Brande

HOW MUCH YOU CAN MAKE WITH A GRINDSTONED NOSE

This is a rough estimate based on writing four episodes a week, keeping this up for a year:

week	word count	cuml words	episodes	cuml episodes	collections	page count	seasons	poss income
1	8000	8000	4	4	1	16		
2	8000	16000	4	8	2	32		
3	8000	24000	4	12	3	48		
4	8000	32000	4	16	4	64	1	
5	8000	40000	4	20	5	80		
6	8000	48000	4	24	6	96		
7	8000	56000	4	28	7	112		
8	8000	64000	4	32	8	128	2	
9	8000	72000	4	36	9	144		
10	8000	80000	4	40	10	160		
11	8000	88000	4	44	11	176		
12	8000	96000	4	48	12	192	3	
13	8000	104000	4	52	13	208		
14	8000	112000	4	56	14	224		
15	8000	120000	4	60	15	240		
16	8000	128000	4	64	16	256	4	
				$22.18	$33.49		$11.17	$66.84
48		384000		192	48	768	12	
				$66.53	$100.46		$33.52	$200.51
								$72,182.88

Note: that's four 2500-word episodes per week for 48 weeks. Shown are the first 16 weeks, and cumulative totals.

Ebooks are priced at $.99 with a 35% royalty, collections are priced at $2.99 with episodes priced at $3.99, both at 70% royalties.

AS SEEN ON TV - THE HISTORY OF SERIALS AS WE'VE WATCHED THEM

As seen on TV, just not on your bookshelf - or is it?

You and I have spent our time and money following "favorite" shows from one season to the next. Like me, you probably have collections on DVD so you can rewatch episodes whenever you feel like it.

Netflix has found that by releasing all of a year's episodes at once, they have helped fuel a fad called binge-watching. This is where an entire season's episodes is viewed over a weekend or during a week. Often binge-watching is organized as a favorite activity with friends, even family.

(FWIW, the Obama's admitted to binge-watching "House of Cards" and "Scandal".)

Wikipedia has "binge watching" as:

> "Binge-watching, also called binge-viewing or marathon-viewing, is the practice of watching television for a long time span, usually of a single television show. In a survey conducted by Netflix in February 2014, 73% of people define binge-watching as "watching between 2-6 episodes of the same TV show in one sitting." Binge-watching as an observed cultural phenomenon has become popular with the rise of online media services such as Netflix, Hulu, and Amazon Video with which the viewer can watch television shows and movies on-demand.

> "History: The idea of assembling several consecutive episodes of a television series in order and watching them in rapid succession originated with the marathon, in which the television stations themselves programmed several hours' worth of reruns of a single series. This practice began in the 1980s and is still popular among subscription television outlets.

> "The usage of the word "binge-watch" can be traced as far back as the late 1990s, when it was used by circles of television fandoms. It has consisted of watching several episodes of a particular show in a row via DVD sets. Prior to the introduction of the DVD format, it was commonplace to record multiple episodes, or even entire miniseries to videotape to watch later in a single viewing session. The word's usage was popularized

with the advent of on-demand viewing and online streaming. In 2013, the word "exploded" into mainstream use when "Netflix started releasing episodes of its serial programming simultaneously. 61% of the Netflix survey participants said that they binge watch regularly."

Why do people binge watch?

They are involved in a serial, which is episodic storytelling. This type of story involves the viewer or reader in the story arcs of recurring characters as they are involved in various situations weekly.

Serials are the oldest form of publication.

Wikipedia has this traced to the 17th century, where the development of movable type made printing affordable to the common person. Books, however, were still expensive and out of the budget of most. Authors found they could write and publish parts of their works and reach a broad audience.

> "During the late 19th century, those that were considered the best American writers first published their work in serial form and then only later in a completed volume format. As a piece in Scribner's Monthly explained in 1878, 'Now it is the second or third rate novelist who cannot get publication in a magazine, and is obliged to publish in a volume, and it is in the magazine that the best novelist always appears first.' Among the American writers that wrote in serial form were Henry James, Harriet Beecher Stowe and Herman Melville. A large part of the appeal for writers at the time was the broad audiences that serialization could reach, which would then grow their following for published works.

> "One of the first significant American works to be released in serial format is Uncle Tom's Cabin, by Harriet Beecher Stowe, which was published over a 40-week period by The National Era, an abolitionist periodical, starting with the June 5, 1851 issue."

This practice continued as it was profitable for both publications and authors up into the late 20th century. At this time, the expansion of broadcast television took most of this market.

Soap Operas as Serials

The American soap opera Guiding Light started as a radio drama in January 1937 and subsequently transferred to television in June 1952.

Guiding Light was heard or seen nearly every weekday since it began, until 2009 making it the longest story ever told in a broadcast medium.

In the name, "soap" refers to the soap and detergent commercials originally broadcast during the shows, which were aimed at women who were cleaning their houses at the time of listening or viewing, and "opera" refers to the melodramatic character of the shows, according to Kate Bowles (from Soap opera: 'No end of story, ever' in The Australian TV Book, pg. 118)

Originally these serial TV shows were broadcast as fifteen-minute installments each weekday in daytime slots. In 1956, As the World Turns and The Edge of Night, both produced by Procter & Gamble Productions, debuted as the first half-hour soap operas.

Again, each story followed the main characters as they dealt with life stories, frequently marital problems. "Romance, secret relationships, extramarital affairs, and genuine love have been the basis for many soap opera storylines. In U.S. daytime serials, the most popular soap opera characters, and the most popular storylines, often involved a romance of the sort presented in paperback romance novels. Soap opera storylines sometimes weave intricate, convoluted and sometimes confusing tales of characters who have affairs, meet mysterious strangers and fall in love, and who commit adultery, all of which keeps audiences hooked on the unfolding story twists." (Again, source: Wikipedia.)

As housewives more frequently entered the workplace, daytime soap operas declined, and popular primetime versions emerged, such as Dallas, Beverly Hills 90210, Desperate Housewives, and Scandal.

Serials as TV and Movie Productions

The over-arcing story has presented problems for TV shows. While avid viewers insist on this format, gaining new viewers is more difficult due to having to "catch up" to what is going on. As video recorders and later DVD releases (as well as the rise of Netflix and online downloads) this has been seen as less of a problem, as they can simply get earlier episodes and entire seasons.

Getting access to DVD's and direct downloads has caused problems in TV ratings, as these are not accessed over TV and so are not counted. Without accurate ratings, selling advertising has become more difficult.

The format for "TV" serials came from the same success they found in print, overarching plots with episodic adventures or stories which were resolved that week, adding to the longer questions of what was happening with the characters to remain unsolved.

With the standard 12 minute breaks in hour-long TV shows (for commercial advertisements) cliffhangers were employed so that viewers had to return to see how the characters resolved that situation. Infrequently, these also ran at the end of an episode, to encourage the viewer to return for the next scheduled episode. At the season finale's, these were often used to hook the viewers with a cliffhanger that could only be resolved in the next season's installments.

A famous episode was "Who Shot J.R.?" on Dallas, where the main character was shot in the final minutes of that season's finale.

HOW THIS BOOK WAS WRITTEN

This book is definitely not a serial.

But it does show that a 1st draft doesn't have to take forever.

The first draft was just over 8200 words long.

It took me something less than 12 hours to get to that point. (Interrupted by having to get some hay bales in before it rained.) And that included doing the research.

The second draft wound up over 10K and took the greater part of the next day.

Which proves the general idea of having 8K worth of serials ready in a week. (That would be nearly 4 serial episodes, or a half-season per our plan. Plus the half-season collection would make 5 books to post on Amazon.) And, as covered, if you wanted to do 8-hour days like Asimov, you could probably do a season of 8 episodes in a week. Your sequence would then be to ship it off for editing, and start on the next. Just like was laid out. Figure in three weeks you could have two seasons ready for publishing. And so, your marketing could start. At that point, the self-publishing indie author reverts back to half-days at marketing and half-days at writing (where you are working on your third season...)

Practice would make this faster. Generally, I can crank out over 2500 words in a couple of hours. Turning this into fiction should make the whole scene faster, as once the research is done for the background and characters of a book, you are then pushing straight through.

The overall scene is to keep to a schedule that would give you a season every two months, which would be 50 singles, 12 half-season collections, 6 season collections, and probably some multi-season collections. Audiobooks have to be added into this, which would take about 2 hours per book to record and produce. Perhaps this could be done on the weekend, or as income improves, farm out completely. Covers can be farmed out, for sure, and done in bulk for the entire season at once.

Again, this gives you the potential to earn income several times what you would make by writing longish novels.

Who knows, maybe it gets picked up for serialization on cable?

One can always dream.

And any dream can be made into reality.

Tools I used:

Computer:

- Ubuntu OS on a dual-CPU vanilla box.
- MAC mini as backup

Software:

- Writing - Scrivener
- Editing and PDF generation - LibreOffice
- Cover - GIMP
- Audio - Audacity and the above computer with a Blue Snowball USB mic.

PS. Obviously, this book calls for a test of that business plan outline. I should take a couple of weeks and try it, then update here on the results. Look for a season of serials to show up soon...

BONUS

Get Access to Writing
and Publishing Materials
from Our Library Collection

Instant Access – Join Here

Click or type into your browser:

http://livesensical.com/go/writingbooks/

www.ingramcontent.com/pod-product-compliance
Lightning Source LLC
Chambersburg PA
CBHW021929170526
45157CB00005B/2252